CLASSIC WISDOM COLLECTION

Today's Questions. Timeless Answers.

Looking for time-tested guidance for the dilemmas of the spiritual life? Find it in the company of the wise spiritual masters of our Catholic tradition.

Comfort in Hardship: Wisdom from Thérèse of Lisieux

Inner Peace: Wisdom from Jean-Pierre de Caussade

Life's Purpose: Wisdom from John Henry Newman

Path of Holiness: Wisdom from Catherine of Siena

Secrets of the Spirit: Wisdom from Luis Martinez

A Simple Life: Wisdom from Jane Frances de Chantal

Solace in Suffering: Wisdom from Thomas à Kempis

Strength in Darkness: Wisdom from John of the Cross

Forthcoming volumes will include wisdom from:
Francis de Sales
Teresa of Avila

A Simple Life

CLASSIC WISDOM COLLECTION

A Simple Life

Wisdom from Jane Frances de Chantal

Edited and with a Foreword by Kathryn Hermes, FSP

Pauline
BOOKS & MEDIA
Boston

Library of Congress Cataloging-in-Publication Data

Chantal, Jeanne-Françoise de, Saint, 1572-1641.
[Selections. English. 2011]
 A simple life : wisdom from Jane Frances de Chantal / edited and
with a foreword by Kathryn Hermes.
p. cm. — (Catholic wisdom collection)
Includes bibliographical references (p. 85).
ISBN 0-8198-7147-8 (pbk.)
 1. Spiritual life—Catholic Church—Early works to 1800. I. Hermes,
Kathryn. II. Title. III. Series.
BX4700.C56A25 2011
248.4'82--dc22

                                        2010043343

Because Saint Jane Frances de Chantal freely quoted Scripture from
memory in her conferences and letters, we have chosen not to change
her Scripture references, and have merely reproduced the translation
of the original French.

Cover design by Rosana Usselmann

Cover photo by Mary Emmanuel Alves, FSP

"P" and PAULINE are registered trademarks of the Daughters of St.
Paul.

Copyright © 2011, Daughters of St. Paul

Published by Pauline Books & Media, 50 Saint Pauls Avenue, Boston,
MA 02130-3491

Printed in the U.S.A.

www.pauline.org

Pauline Books & Media is the publishing house of the Daughters of
St. Paul, an international congregation of women religious serving
the Church with the communications media.

1 2 3 4 5 6 7 8 9   15 14 13 12 11

Contents

Foreword

It is a blessed moment when one discovers a kindred spirit among the saints. When this happens, it often becomes apparent that the spiritual friendship had been developing quietly and patiently throughout life, waiting for the moment when it would blossom into a kinship of soul. In my regard, such a friend has been Saint Jane Frances de Chantal. As a teenager, I met her indirectly when I made a vocational retreat at the Georgetown Monastery of the Sisters of the Visitation, an order she founded in France during the seventeenth century together with Saint Francis de Sales. Shortly after my religious profession as a Daughter of Saint Paul, our paths crossed again when I read *Abandonment to Divine Providence*, a book by an eighteenth-century Jesuit spiritual director of the

Visitation nuns at Nancy, France. His spiritual counsel for the nuns often referred to the words of their foundress, Jane de Chantal. A few years later, as I began to take on more responsibility in the mission of my community, Saint Jane's counsels on contemplative prayer to her Daughters in the Visitation monasteries responded to my own thirst for a deeper prayer life.

Recently, however, at another turning point in my midlife years, I have found my spiritual landscape painted with the colors of Jane de Chantal's spirit. Now, as I read about her spiritual journey, her friendship with Francis de Sales, and their founding of the Visitation sisters, I find that she is tying together the loose ends of my varied experiences, pointing out the path that both our souls have taken.

Jane Frances Frémyot de Chantal was born in 1572 in Dijon, France. When she was twenty she married the Baron Christophe de Rabutin-Chantal. It was a happy marriage; however, the couple had to deal with the problem of Christophe's occasional infidelity. Jane reared and educated their three daughters and one son, as well as the daughter Christophe had out of wedlock, Claudine de Chantal. Jane proved to be a capable administrator of the household and estates. But in 1601 their marriage ended tragically when Christophe was mortally wounded while hunting with a friend. His friend's gun strap caught on a protruding branch, and the weapon went off, scattering shot, some of which hit Christophe. For nine days Christophe prepared himself and his wife for his death. He insisted that she make peace with this and never speak against his unhappy friend. Nevertheless, Jane was inconsolable and mourned his death deeply for many years. During this period of mourning she began to sense a call to a new way of life. Her life, like the pieces of a jigsaw puzzle, had been thrown down and no longer fit together as they once had. Desires for an intimacy greater even than what she had experienced with Christophe filled her soul with restless yearning. She made a private vow of chastity and began searching for a director who could help her follow the way God seemed to be indicating to her. Her first director tied her down to a rigid spiritual discipline. However, in 1604 she met the young bishop of Geneva, Francis de Sales, while he was giving a Lenten retreat. She felt that this man was the one who could help her discover the secret of what was flowering within her and help her move from the nebulous impulses she felt in her soul to a new vision of life.

When Francis heard Jane's confession, he sensed something special about this woman. After prayer he agreed to become Jane's spiritual director and very gently began to accompany the young widow to spiritual freedom and maturity. At the foundation of her spiritual growth was the Salesian belief that to be a Christian is to be a fully realized human being. To be fully human is to become the lovers of God we are meant to be. This is the goal of what Francis calls the "devout life." To accomplish this growth we must walk the parallel paths of complete trust in God's goodness and radical surrender to whatever events or states we experience in life. So Jane first had to learn to love her widowhood without racing past it for something seemingly better. As Francis guided her, she learned to live her life with gentle patience, without knowing the next step. She continued her custom of nursing the sick, rearing and educating her children, practicing a quiet meditation on the mysteries of Christ, and desiring nothing other than what life handed her at that moment. Jane wanted to get on with her life, but the Genevan bishop kept her right where she was. The lessons she learned from Francis's guidance would form the bedrock of her contemplative teaching later in life.

The widow whose life was beginning to deepen still struggled with unresolved anger toward the friend who had accidentally killed her husband. Francis knew her struggles, for she revealed to him all the movements and grapplings of her soul. He instructed her not to seek the unfortunate man out, but if he were to come to Jane she was to receive him with a compassionate and gracious heart. Her blood might boil and she might be agitated and uneasy, but emotions only prove that we are human. What counted was the decision of her will to treat him gently. Saint Francis wanted her to discover that she was capable of loving all things, even the death of her husband, through the death of Jesus our Savior. She was to learn to love all that life presented to her, to be compassionate beyond her present capacity, to embrace all crosses.

Indeed, Salesian spirituality holds that the interior life is a continuous "denudation" or a stripping of the self so that the presence of God can be most perfectly realized. Jane learned to detach her heart from all things, so that, emptied of self-will, her life might manifest the will of God. Her days were filled not with heroic spiritual feats but with the practice of the hidden virtues of humility, patience, transparency, simplicity, meekness of heart, and cheerful bearing with others.

In 1607 Saint Francis de Sales confided to the Baroness de Chantal his dream of founding monasteries for "daughters of prayer" who would practice the hidden virtues he had taught her, while living in the presence of God. Jane at once realized that this was what she had been yearning for. Together these two friends founded the first Monastery of the Visitation of Holy Mary at Annecy, France, in 1610, and by the time of her death Jane had been instrumental in the foundation of more than eighty monasteries of the Visitation. The new order drank deeply from the well of her contemplative spirit. She taught her Daughters to rest in the spirit of God and leave all else aside. Her counsels on prayer, included in this book, break open the experiences of her long "waiting" years for her Daughters as well as for the many people who asked her advice. Even Saint Francis de Sales, who directed her until his death, learned contemplation from the school of her prayer. She died in 1641.

———— ❧ ————

Saint Jane Frances de Chantal lived in the time of transition between the medieval and modern worlds. It was a time of violence and intolerance. It saw the Reformation, which shook the foundations of society, and the birth of a more militant Church in the Counter-Reformation. She was not a simple nun withdrawn from the world; rather, she played out her life as a mother, administrator, foundress, teacher, contemplative, and spiritual director. In a world not so unlike our own, she was an ordinary woman who shows us that it is possible to love the impossible and embrace the unbearable. She and Francis de Sales undertook the spiritual revitalization of their society through "the devout life." Their way of prayer and path to inner maturity speak to the thirst for the spiritual that drives so many people today, though they may slake that thirst far from the Church. In today's world, novelty and consumerism daily manipulate our desires. Jane's example of pursuing inner unity of life in following the will of God offers rest to our psyche. In the midst of the spirit of personal entitlement that lies under our demands, Jane encourages us to seek humility, meekness of heart, gracious cordiality, and regard for one another. Today we are victims of and witnesses to violence at a new level. Saint Jane herself also suffered from the effects of anger, sorrow, and pain, and she attracts us with gentle counsel to live in harmony with God's will without ifs, buts, or exceptions. Jane wanted but one place from which to view all events—the love of a trustworthy God.

Finally, Jane taught a lesson that is most precious to me at this time in my life, one that I personally thank her for: the great affection that she had for her Sisters of the Visitation. Her counsels radiate this affection, as you will see. Today we drown in sentiment and emotion yet wonder why we are so lonely, so empty. Jane's friendship with Francis de Sales and her affection and goodness toward her "Daughters" who followed her in the Visitation

Order, teach us a way of friendship and prayer that is pure, simple, and humble, which seeks the others' good in Jesus. With her there is no holding back. Her love for others is as strong as her love for God. Indeed, they cannot be separated.

In the end, the path of Jane's life has played itself out in my own—different events, different situations, but the same call to unity of life in trusting the fidelity of God. Jane now walks with me as I ask myself midlife questions about meaning and fulfillment. Her teaching and her very life show that in the process of living the Christian life, of becoming Christ-ed, we are turned inside out by life events we cannot control. We are destroyed and remade. This process, and none other, brings all our talents and resources to full maturity. Is this new life what you are longing for?

I

Desire Only God

Saint Jane's advice to the Visitation Sisters at Nevers:

A soul abandoned completely to Divine Providence desires only God and is detached from all but him: there is no eventuality that can unsettle her. Nothing so strips the soul and gives it greater dependence on God than the practice of the maxim of our blessed Father, Francis de Sales: *Ask for nothing and refuse nothing*.

In answer to a question from one of her Daughters on how to make a good beginning in the spiritual life, Saint Jane says:

Distrust yourselves, despise yourselves; it is the only way of laying a good foundation. Nothing else is needed, except to do so with complete trust in God. I think the reason why we see so little solid virtue is that people are not thoroughly instructed in this principle. There is so much speculation, so much account made of high ways of prayer, of transports, of things intangible, outside of and beyond the common way. Yet trust in God and distrust of self are what constitute holiness and true virtue. Humility is nothing else than the contempt and putting aside of self; it is the love of one's own effacement, miseries, abjection; the gentle bearing with; even the wishing sweetly, cheerfully, and lovingly that we should be held and treated for what we are.

But you say: How can a soul that is very imperfect and full of miseries have this generous confidence? Our blessed Father was fond of saying that the weaker he felt the more strength and confidence he had, inasmuch as he expected nothing from himself and placed all his trust in God. He was so glad when anyone fell into faults of frailty because he held it good for humbling the soul and showing the futility of trusting to self and the value of grace, of God's help. Indeed such souls should have great courage to take in hand their perfection, without being astonished or troubled in the least on seeing they are subject to so many faults and frailties.

Saint Jane's answer to a question about the counsel of Saint Francis de Sales, "Ask for nothing and refuse nothing":

We are not to ask for nor refuse those things that are purely indifferent, which only self-love would make us desire or refuse. Undoubtedly souls adopt an admirable practice who live prepared for whatever God wishes to do with them and in them, unconcerned about everything except to abide near him, to do and to suffer faithfully whatever his Providence puts in their way at each moment. However, others, instead of being attentive to God and their duty, think only about themselves and are caught between the desire of pursuing convenience and the fear of going against the counsel to ask for nothing and to refuse nothing. These I advise by all means to go ahead and ask humbly and simply and as soon as possible for what they think they require. The counsel to ask for nothing and to refuse nothing is assuredly a counsel of very high perfection. Our blessed Father has given it to us as an abridgment of the means of attaining this perfection, for it is nothing short of the practice of perfect renunciation and indifference.

— Excerpts from a conference given to the Sisters of the Visitation at Nevers, France, a conference given to the Sisters of the Visitation, and an undated letter written to an unknown recipient

II

Perfect Simplicity

Referring to Saint Francis's favorite maxim for acquiring perfection, "Ask for nothing and refuse nothing," Saint Jane says:

Few things are needed for perfection: to will what is right and to do it—everything lies in this. But it is rare indeed to find one who will take up in real earnest and with determination the complete renunciation of self this entails.

Perfect simplicity, my Daughters, consists in having one single aim in all our actions: that of pleasing God. The second practice follows upon this: to see only the will of God in everything good or ill that befalls us. Then whatsoever the event we shall always be tranquil because we shall have no love, no desire other than that of his adorable will. Then we shall be at peace even if some happening may [apparently] delay our perfection at which, nevertheless, we shall not cease to toil. The third practice entailed by this virtue is to bare our faults with the utmost candor [before those who guide us]. The fourth is to be truthful in our speech, not multiplying our words especially when there is question of justifying ourselves. The fifth is to commit ourselves to Divine Providence with entire trust, living from day to day with neither forethought nor care for ourselves, but doing well at each moment what we are ordered to do according to our vocation. If we faithfully make use of occasions as they present themselves we may be certain that God, for his glory and our sanctification, will not fail to provide us with greater opportunities.

It is impossible to be truly simple and at the same time have so many cares for the future. Genuine simplicity hinders reflections on our actions and makes us artless. If our actions are good we have no need to consider them; if they are imperfect our heart will surely tell us; and if we expose them to those who direct us they will have the judgment to distinguish. I consider it an act of great perfection to conform ourselves in all things to the community and from this never of our own choice to desist. Even more, this is so good a way of becoming united to our neighbor, as well as an excellent means of hiding one's perfection from oneself. In this practice is to be found a certain simplicity of heart that contains absolutely all perfection. This sacred simplicity enables the soul to live within herself in order to apply herself wholly and solely to the love of her supreme good. She effects this by the simple observance of her Rule without effusive desires to look elsewhere for perfection. She seeks not to achieve striking things that might bring upon her the esteem of others; she keeps herself in lowliness and self-abasement. She has no great satisfactions, because she does nothing wherein she can find them, nothing more than the community, nothing, it seems to her, of any profit. And in this way the knowledge of her holiness is hidden from her. God alone sees it, and she ravishes his heart by this divine simplicity, uniting herself to him by a perfectly pure, perfectly simple, perfectly loyal love. She no longer heeds the suggestions of self-love, no longer listens to its persuasions, and no longer is concerned about her own views or methods, which by conspicuous actions or great undertakings might win her distinction.

Such a soul enjoys an abiding peace; she can say that she is free by divine union to rise above herself. Therefore, my Daughters, never think that you are doing something insignificant by following life in common.

— Excerpt from a conference given to the Sisters of the Visitation

III

Surrender Yourself Absolutely

Saint Jane's words to her Daughters on how God watches over them:

Usually God draws to great renunciation those who earnestly seek to purify their hearts, and of these souls he takes particular care.

If, when the Church is keeping her great liturgical feasts, you should be drawn to the prayer of simplicity, let it not disquiet you that your mind is not occupied with the mystery of the day, for you must always follow where you are being drawn by God. However, outside the time of prayer we may read or think about the feast being celebrated, for, although we were to have but a few thoughts regarding the feast, we feel within us certain sweet longings to be accordant with it, certain feelings of joy or the like. But, for prayer itself, the secret is always to follow the attraction given to us. Oh, my God, how many souls are oftentimes troubled about their prayer, doubting if they pray correctly, and yet to pray as he draws them is all God asks.

Of a truth, Daughters, it is a consolation without compare to surrender oneself absolutely to God and to be conscious that he sees and penetrates the most hidden secrets of our heart. This is a good way of keeping oneself in his presence.

Souls drawn to the prayer of simplicity should be most careful to curtail a certain eagerness that creates a desire to be active during the time of our prayer. It is pure self-love that breeds this hankering, and it deprives us of simple attention and occupation to the presence of God.

A good practice of simplicity, much recommended by our blessed Father, is to make but few reflections on the past, the future, or even the present, but instead to ask counsel of God by raising our thoughts to him, be it on our way to the parlor or for other matters of our charge. Our Lord taught me this practice long ago and I recommend it to you.

In our communion with our Lord we should find all our delight, caring not whether it is his good pleasure to give us consolation or desolation. This absolute dependence on and conformity to the will of God is the sum and root of perfection. . . . The whole doctrine of our blessed Father tends to perfect denudation of self. . . . We are all called to this perfection, and to attain to it there is no need to weaken the body by penances and austerities. We are, therefore, without excuse if we fail to practice it. Indeed, the absolute and complete surrender of our whole being to the will of God—this reposing in the care of his Providence—is the greatest assurance of salvation we can have in this life. Repose is very easy, sweet, comfortable, and pleasant, but to surrender ourselves without abandoning or hindering his holy will is far higher, greater, and more exalted, because it means perfect indifference to everything so long as it is the will of God.

— Excerpt from a conference given to the Sisters of the Visitation

IV

Preparation for Prayer

Saint Jane counsels her Daughters on the difficulties to be expected in the practice of prayer and the manner of dealing with them:

The first advice for the soul who would pray and who is not drawn by any unusual attraction or elevation of the spirit to God, is to prepare herself diligently according to the saying of the wise man, *Before prayer prepare your soul; think where you are going and to whom you speak.*

Mental prayer is often badly made solely for want of due preparation. This preparation is twofold: remote and immediate. Remote preparation consists in keeping the conscience in tranquility, in guarding the senses, in fostering an ordinary perception of God and intimate inward converse with his Divine Majesty. But more essential than all these ways is the emancipation of the soul from all immoderate affections and passions. In a word, she should renounce every disturbing influence of mind or conscience that might hamper her inward liberty and recollection.

Mortification and prayer are the two wings of the dove by which she takes flight into holy solitude, there to find her repose with God, far from the haunts of men. As birds cannot soar on high with only one wing, neither should the soul persuade herself that she can rise aloft to God by mortification unless it be accompanied by prayer. Mortification without prayer is useless toil, and prayer without mortification is like meat without salt, it soon corrupts. Hence must the soul provide herself with both wings if her flight is to be towards the courts of heaven where her heart ought to find its full content in converse with God.

We must, my Daughters, strip ourselves of all things, absolutely. We must bravely renounce every created thing by letting self-denial dominate our lives, making ourselves master of our passions, trampling under foot their rebellion. Our own will must be subject to constraint; our own judgment supple, willing, dependent on God in all that regards our inward life. Once the Holy Spirit has made himself Master of the soul, the great method of prayer is to have none, for in her he then acts with a free hand and there is no longer need of rules and methods.

Prayer is the work of grace and not any contrivance of our own. Begin prayer by faith, remain in it by hope, and come forth from it in that charity that only asks to do and suffer. In a word, the heart must be stripped bare and in all ways detached; the soul, as far as her energies admit, naked in the sight of God with complete submission of self to his designs, sometimes even formally renewing the resolution to this effect.

On fidelity to grace, Saint Jane says:

Our Holy Mother Church defines that grace never fails us, never leaves us unless we leave it. Our good God waits patiently for us when we procrastinate, but if we go on indefinitely rejecting him and will not receive him, the Spirit of God departs, leaves us. Holy Scripture testifies to this in many places. When the Bridegroom has earnestly entreated his spouse to open the door to him and she continues making excuses, this Sacred Lover passes on, and when later she changes her mind and opens the door to him she finds him no more (cf. Song

5:2–6). My dear Sisters, when we feel urged to shake off some sin, to quit an imperfection, to acquire a virtue, to make rapid strides to the perfection of divine love, then the hour is come for us, let us arise in haste. Let us run to the Divine Spouse, accept his grace, profit by his inspiration. It is the hour of deliverance. Let us not tarry, let us run, let us be swift-footed. My dear Daughters, that God would withdraw his inspirations would be for us the misfortune of misfortunes.

Oh, my Daughters, when by our negligence we cease to profit by these precious and divine inspirations we may justly fear that the propitious time will not return to us. *A time will come,* says our Lord, *when you shall seek me and shall not find me, you shall call and I will not answer* (cf. Jn 7:34). "And why is this so, Lord?" "Because when I sought you again and again, when I asked time after time for you, you hid from me and would not answer me. I have shown myself to you and you had no desire to look upon me, now I will treat you in like manner."

Correspond, my Daughters, to these divine attractions no matter what the cost, for *Heaven suffers violence and the violent bear it away* (cf. Mt 11:12).

— Excerpts from conferences on prayer
given to the Sisters of the Visitation

V

Fidelity in Prayer

Fidelity of soul consists in being perfectly resigned to the will of God, in enduring whatever his goodness permits to happen to us, in doing all our spiritual exercises in love and for love, above all the exercise of prayer. Prayer is a pure elevation of our minds to God, believing that he is more in us than we are in ourselves. Our success in prayer depends on this and not on discourse and considerations, of which if we are deprived we need not be troubled. Neither should we be troubled when we sleep at prayer, provided we resist it. Let us patiently suffer it and keep ourselves before God as a statue to receive all he sends (cf. Saint Francis de Sales, *On the Love of God*, Book 6: Chapter

11). It gives our Lord pleasure to see us fighting sleep all the time of prayer. We must bear with it and love our abjection.

Prayer is a hidden manna, neither known or valued, save by those to whom it is given, and the more we taste it the more does our appetite for it grow. . . . A soul who has this spirit of prayer does more work in one hour than another, who is without it, will do in many; and her work done, she hastens to converse with her God, for this is her repose. However, it is only to the obedient that God thus communicates himself.

Careful examination of conscience is a practical method of prayer by which we get to know ourselves, to acquire humility, to purify our heart—all important dispositions for familiar conversation with God. At the end of prayer we should likewise examine our conscience.

No virtue is perfect that has not been tested by one's neighbor. Were he to hold our kinsfolk, our brethren in religion, or other of our friends in dishonor we must simply suffer the reproach. The afflictions of the divine service such as aridity, distractions, darkness, timidity, scruples, temptations, persecutions of the devil, or trials caused by confessors or by ministers of God we must bear without murmur, because they are God's good pleasure. Those who persevere in the endurance of them, will, at last, be admitted to the surpassing sweetness of the intimate ways of the prayer of union with God, and then they will be amply rewarded.

From some persons God holds back these favors, either because they are a prey to vices, each one of which is a dark cloud shutting out from the soul the sight of the Creator, or more often, to make them understand the excellence of what they seek, by the long-drawn-out time that has to be devoted to their attainment.

Meanwhile God tests the soul in many ways both by inward and outward trials, and so by experiencing how dearly it costs, we learn to value the great prize for which we run.

In prayer we should freely unburden ourselves to God, telling him, our Lord and Master, in the most familiar and confidential way, everything, great and small, of heaven or of earth, much or little. We should open our heart, pouring it all out to him without reserve; recounting its burdens, its sins, its aspirations; revealing our whole self; seeking repose in his company as with a friend on whom one relies and to whom one confides both the good and the bad. This is what Holy Scripture calls *pouring out his heart like water in the divine presence* (cf. Lam 2:19), manifesting not only those things that are of great importance but even the most insignificant of things.

Seeing that Divine Providence governs all and that we can do nothing without its assistance, it is wise to confer with God, for whatever good comes to us in any way, it comes from him.

Let there be no timidity in our supplications; he does not like it.

— Excerpt from conferences on prayer given to the Sisters of the Visitation

VI

Tranquility of Heart

Saint Jane speaks to her Daughters on prayer, and on signs of true inspiration and holy indifference:

Do what the Lord counsels you. The souls who are prompt in following the divine inspirations are those whom the Eternal Father has prepared to be the spouses of his Beloved Son. We must go where inspiration urges us, without flinching. Having found the will of God in our vocation we remain lovingly in its practice. A good sign of a true inspiration, and more especially of an extraordinary inspiration, is tranquility of heart. Peace is inseparable from most holy humility. I speak of a humility that is noble, real, that reaches to the very marrow, is solid, supple to correction, pliable, and prompt to obedience. In a word, the three best marks of a legitimate inspiration are: perseverance against inconstancy and levity, a tranquil heart against anxiety and over-eagerness, humble obedience against obstinacy and capriciousness.

In order to find out what is sound in a matter of inspiration, we should get the advice of a wise spiritual father, and if he fails, consult two or three spiritual persons. Then make a decision and in the name of God adhere to your resolve, taking heed to progress in it and to act up to it perseveringly.

Although difficulties, temptations, and the vicissitudes of events meet us in our progress, we must hold to our decision and not let them affect it, considering that if we had made another choice we should perhaps find it a hundred times worse. After we have made a decision with a devout mind we must no longer doubt the holiness of carrying it out. If we persevere in it, it will never fail us; to do otherwise is a mark of great self-love, childishness, or a shallow mind.

God, oftentimes, to exercise us in holy indifference, inspires us with great projects in which, however, he does not wish us to succeed. Thus, as we ought boldly, courageously, and perseveringly to begin and to continue the work as long as we are able, so must we gently and tranquilly acquiesce in the issue of the enterprise, whatever it may please God that it should be. Oh, how blessed are such souls, valiant and strong in undertaking the enterprise with which God inspires them, gentle and supple in laying it down when God so wills. Such are the marks of a very perfect indifference. We, on the contrary, wish that whatever we have undertaken should succeed; yet it is unreasonable to expect that God should do everything to our liking.

In a letter to M. Noël Brulart (Commandeur de Sillery) at a time when, due to strong opposition, he was forced to abandon a far-reaching work of charity, Saint Jane writes:

Our blessed Father used to say that we should with firm, unshakable, long-winded courage, without ever growing slack, pursue the good works committed to us by God so long as we see his holy will in them. But he said also that we should, if such were God's good pleasure, cease the pursuit, and even more than that, if it did not succeed, sweetly and tranquilly abandon it altogether.

— Excerpts from conferences on prayer given to the
Sisters of the Visitation; from a letter written to
M. Noël Brulart (Commandeur de Sillery), July 18, 1638

VII

How to Meditate

Saint Jane continues her advice to her Daughters on prayer:

Prayer is one of the most efficacious means of glorifying God, but Saint Gregory teaches us that there are temperaments so restless that they are incapable of the repose necessary for mental prayer. These must first be taught to practice the virtues, vocal prayer, and other devotions, until little by little they learn to subdue their nature and later, by these means, somewhat fit themselves for prayer. God gives devotion to those who sincerely plead with him for the grace of contrition, and to those who conquer their temptations and passions he will give the hidden manna of prayer.

In prayer we should interrogate our hearts as to whether or not we possess the virtue or the vice upon which we meditate. If the passion of Jesus Christ be the subject of our meditation, let us say to our Lord: What fear or what interest induced you to endure such cruel torments? And straightway he will answer: Not fear, because I am omnipotent; not interest, because I am God. It was my love for you alone that impelled me.

At this word, "love," the soul will stay her questioning because it will awaken love within her own heart until she is drawn and impelled to say that for love of him she will suffer oblivion, contempt, bitterness, and similar hard things repugnant to nature.

Now to meditate with profit we must be mindful to ponder and weigh [the cost of] the reformation of our actions against those which Jesus Christ has done and suffered. . . . The highest science of prayer and the greatest profit lie in suffering and humiliating ourselves rather than in feeling relish and consolations.

When the love of created things tries to draw away the mind and makes us disobedient to the Divine Majesty, the great, divine love within the soul takes the lead as another Saint Michael and captures its powers and senses for the service of God by the intrepid words, *Who is like God?*

This love of God should be the motivating power of all—wide in its expansion, surpassing all other loves, conquering all difficulties, choosing the highest honor and the good pleasure of God, above all else, absolutely, with no reservation.

O true God! How often for the satisfaction of trifles, illusions, vain and unsubstantial things do we forsake the love of our heavenly Spouse! How then can we say that we love him above all things when we prefer such inane vanities to his grace? *They have forsaken me,* said God, *I who am the fountain of living water and have dug for themselves cisterns, broken cisterns, that can hold no water* (cf. Jer 2:13). It is, then, for love of us that he wishes we should love him, because we cannot cease to love him without a loss to ourselves, and by every affection that we take away from him we lose him.

Believe me, my Daughters, we must bring to prayer all the tranquility of heart we can possibly command and shut ourselves up in the little heaven that is within us, shutting out all objects of sense and firmly believing that we shall not fail *to drink of the water from the cistern.*

The hour of prayer having come, the soul who with holy impatience awaits that happy moment ought straightway to answer the signal and hasten to receive the honor about to be conferred upon her. She should then invoke the Holy Spirit, the Blessed Virgin, her good angel, and such saints as she may choose to help her in her prayer and to remain with her while she is before God. She should gather together all her powers and say to herself: My soul, you are about to appear before God to hold converse with him—a truce to all else.

To enter into the presence of God let us sometimes represent him to ourselves as filling the whole universe, thinking of him as omnipresent like the air we breathe. Again, we may look upon God as surrounding us on every side, we being in him as fish are in the sea or birds in the air. Or we may withdraw into our inward selves and then with a calm, unwavering gaze look upon the Divine Essence as filling our soul and our very being, even as the Father, contemplating himself in his own being, generates the Divine Son from whom, with him, proceeds the Holy Spirit. We may, at other times, fix our thoughts upon Jesus Christ in the Blessed Sacrament of the altar and reflect, as faith teaches us, that in it our Lord in his sacred humanity abides and that this same humanity is seated at the right hand of the Eternal Father. And lastly we must ever humble ourselves and acknowledge that we are unworthy to speak to God, saying with Abraham: *I will speak to my Lord whereas I am but dust and ashes* (cf. Gen 18:27).

We should end our prayer by three acts: thanksgiving, oblation, and petition; this last act is to ask God's help that we may carry out the good resolves that we have made. Let us then gather a little bouquet of devotion from the principal affections we have had, so that its fragrance may permeate the whole day.

— Excerpt from conferences on prayer given
to the Sisters of the Visitation

VIII

The Touch of God

If during prayer the soul feels the touch of God, by which he lets her know that he wishes to communicate with her, she should at once cease from all efforts and await his coming, not hindering it by making vocal or mental acts in prayer, which are now out of place, thus preparing an inward silence to receive him. She may, however, at times, upon feeling his approach say, *Speak Lord, your servant is listening* (cf. 1 Sam 3:10), and then with tranquility open wide her heart and yield it up to the infusion of grace, which afterward she must turn to good account according to the impulse received in prayer.

Let us tie ourselves down to prayer and never quit it, for in this game (so to say) she is the loser who gives up her prayer. If it seems to you that you are not heard, cry out the louder; if you are driven out one door, come in by another. If you hear the words said to the Canaanite woman, that you do not deserve the graces for which you ask, humbly reply that like her you do not aspire to unusual favors, but only to eat the crumbs that fall from the divine table (cf. Mt 15:22–28).

As God is in an infinitely exalted sphere, if the soul is to attain to him, she must tend upward. The Spouse in the Song of Songs speaking of his bride occupied in prayer compares her to a column of smoke rising towards heaven. Nothing, as she ascends, is able to impede her progress.

Let us realize, dear Daughters, the honor that is ours in being at liberty to pray as frequently and as secretly as we will. Unless we pray from the heart it is not prayer at all, but if we pray from the heart we shall never want for anything.

We need not wonder at seeing those who give themselves up to prayer make small account of earthly things, because being with God they look down from so great a height that they all but lose sight of earthly things.

Saint John Climacus tells us that prayer is the salvation of the world, the office of the angels, the source of grace, and a person's most noble possession, meaning thereby that, possessing so great a good, a person is indifferent to all else. It matters little what God works in the soul because she ought not to be attached to the work of God in her but to the God who works. Having learned from our Lord to enter into herself and to yearn for his presence in her heart, she might, I think, choose rather to endure for a time the pains of hell than return to the pleasures, or, to speak more accurately, to the monotony, the weariness of the world. The more we empty ourselves of all that is not God, the more he fills us with himself. Let us then give up the thought of self that he may take our care upon himself.

The soul has attained the silence of the mystic when she no longer speaks to creatures, or even to God, but with profound inward attention simply listens to him. This silence honors him in a very sublime manner, and by diverting her attention from creatures (thus enabling her freely to apply herself to God, the one source of her purity), it becomes the means of untold good to the soul. We read in Holy Scripture: *Hear, O Israel and be still* (cf. Deut 27:9). Let us then be silent with creatures and listen to God. One word from him to us is worth ten thousand from us to him. He communicates himself spiritually, reaching by his inspirations the deepest depths of the heart, uniting himself to us in an ineffably gentle manner. All is summed up in this: Whoever delivers herself over to God becomes one same spirit with God.

Drown yourself in this ocean of sanctity, of infinite purity, for in such depths he who is lost is the winner. Take my word for it. Daughters dear, the Divine Heart will never fail us if we do not fail him, and even if we do, not even then will he fail us because his loyalty far outweighs our disloyalty.

— Excerpt from conferences on prayer given
to the Sisters of the Visitation

IX

Let the Heart Speak

There is a prayer of the soul's tranquil attention to God that tends to moderate the excessive activity of her faculties and creates an inward silence and repose. Ah, how much better it would often be to listen to God deep down in our heart than to speak to him with our lips.

Then there is a prayer wherein the soul is calm and tranquil, not praying actively, yet nevertheless, she is ready to embrace whatever God may will to do with her, and this love of the will of God is the food of the soul. Again, there is the prayer in which the soul applies herself to God with all her faculties and yet can render to herself no account of how she is occupied. And yet again, there is the prayer of combat and strife made under the pressure of some continuous and violent temptation. Such prayer demands great fidelity to God and a quiet, simple diversion of thought from the subject of pain.

If the mind can say nothing, let the heart speak. Though we had nothing else to say to God than to tell him that we love him and that he is worthy of love, that is enough. The angels in heaven utter but one word, *Sanctus*. In the abode of bliss that is their whole, their solitary prayer. God is both light and darkness to each one as he sees fit. If he is darkness to you, seek nothing else. There is more reverence in humbly abasing oneself in the presence of a mystery than in lifting oneself up to contemplate it with the intellect.

Faith is the light of the new spiritual world; it is the science of the saints. In prayer, then, we should listen rather than speak. It is more fitting to listen to the Son of God than to address him—we, who are not worthy to speak in his presence. Let us leave to him the choice of the discourse, or seek for words within ourselves. But only to the recollected soul does he communicate himself.

Should you then, you ask, remain idle and unoccupied in prayer? No, my Daughters, we must subject our mind to the Holy Spirit who wishes to be its light and its guide. Were you able to do nothing else except remain in the presence of God and consume your life before him as a taper consumes and burns itself out before the Blessed Sacrament, would you not be only too happy?

To be little in his sight is not enough, we must be *nothing*—this is the foundation upon which he would build, because it pleases him to work on nothingness. The greater our annihilation, the loftier the building he erects thereon. When you are at prayer you must neither see nor hear anything but God; even if an angel were to present himself before you, you should take no heed of him, for you are speaking to God, who is greater than he.

Prove to God that you love him not for his rewards but for himself.

If seeing us utterly destitute of all created things allures God to come to our help, will he not be still more willing to succor us when it is he himself who has deprived us of his sensible presence? Well, then, what does it matter if we seem to be forsaken by God provided that we are heard by him? Great should be our joy when for love of him we are cut off from all that is in heaven or on earth and even from God himself for love of himself; then we can say, *What have I in heaven and what do I desire on earth besides you, O my God?* (Ps 73:25).

— Excerpt from conferences on prayer given
to the Sisters of the Visitation

X

Abide in Peace

God weans the souls that are his, first, from the pleasure received from the senses; second, from the lights of reason; third, from the help they receive from persons of piety; fourth, from sensible devotion. Fifth and lastly, God permits these souls, dear to his heart, to fall into states in which it seems to them they are wholly deprived of peace and trust in him. Then it is that those beloved of God find nothing but bitterness in outward things. Reason, with all its stratagems, serves only to augment their troubles; human aid appears to them of no avail; and inward peace fails them at the time they think they most require it. To be in these straits is very profitable to the soul, to the point that, being absolutely destitute and cast adrift from all created aids, God may be its light, its life, its pleasure, its relief, its vesture, its repose, its all. Loving submission to the will of God in inward sufferings is of greater help in developing a more intimate union [with him] than is the solace of relieving ourselves by speaking of our trouble.

⚬

Abide in peace in your state of utter denudation. Blessed are the poor, for God will reclothe them. Oh, how happy should we be if our hearts were stripped bare of all that is not God, and how we should love this poverty and despoliation! To be in darkness, no flavor in our lives, no good sentiments; deprived of all spiritual enlightenment, all help, all satisfaction, no friend to whom we can turn; how desirable is this state! O my Daughter, when the soul finds herself come to this pass, what is left to her but to do as the little unfledged bird that hides itself and cuddles under the wings of good mother Providence, not venturing to come out of cover for fear of being captured by the kite? Such is the refuge where you now find shelter. What is there to fear then? How could you be better off, with what richer vesture could you be clothed than the shelter of the most sweet and paternal Providence of your heavenly Father? Abide as you are, quite content in the possession of this unique treasure. You know you are in my heart and none can ever displace you.

———— ⚘ ————

When God deigns to speak to a soul, all creatures must cease to do so. And this favor I see is yours through divine mercy. You must adhere to this practice of looking at God within you, and it will absorb all others. Let him act according to his good pleasure so that whether he gives you sweet or bitter, satisfaction or dissatisfaction, it may be all one to you. Give little thought to either, but only to him, following faithfully and simply the light he will give you for your good in each event. Let him act, and you will see how he will strip you of everything till there is nothing that you care for save communion with him. May his divine goodness keep you in this way, even unto the utmost perfection of his holy love. Be joyous and brave, I beg of you, and you will experience how sweet God is. Pray for me.

> — Excerpts from conferences on prayer given to the Sisters of the Visitation, an undated letter written to Sister Bonne-Marie de Haraucount, and an undated letter written to Sister Marie Susanne Duret

XI

Cry Out, *Draw Me!*

Saint Jane's advice to her Daughters on prayer, in the context of her reflections on the Song of Songs:

My dear Daughters, we ourselves do not know how to take one step forward in the holy science of prayer. So it is that the sacred spouse in the Song of Songs cries out in her incapability, *Draw me*, that is to say, take the first step, for I cannot of myself arise, but when you shall have aroused me, then, dear Spouse of my soul, I will run. You will run before me, alluring me always on and on, and I, I will follow you in the race, yielding to your attractions. Such is the way in which you will draw me by *the odor of your perfumes* (cf. Song 1:3).

We cannot express, my dear Daughters, the Savior's longing desire to come into our souls. *Open to me,* he says, *my sister, my love, my dove, my undefiled, for my head is full of dew and my locks of the drops of the night* (cf. Song 5:2). Ah! The Divine Lover would say to our souls: I am weighed down with the sufferings and sweat of my passion; open then your heart to me and I will drop into it the dew of my passion, which will be converted into pearls of consolation. The true lover knows no pleasure except in the beloved. Therefore, all things seemed like dross and mire to the glorious Saint Paul in comparison to his Savior, and so it is with the sacred spouse. She gives herself wholly to her Beloved and to him alone. *My Beloved is mine and I am his* (cf. Song 2:16). Should creatures, however excellent, get in her way—even were they angels—she would not linger with them unless they could help her find him whom she seeks. *Tell me, I adjure you, have you seen him whom my soul loves?* (cf. Song 3:3).

O God, if we saw him as he is, we should die of love for him. If we saw his divine heart as he sings the canticle in praise of the Divinity with a voice of infinite sweetness, our hearts would fairly burst with joy. He invites us, this dear friend of our souls. *Arise,* he says, *come out of yourself, take wing towards me, my love, my dove, my beautiful one* (cf. Song 2:10). Come into this celestial abode where all is joy, where all breathe only praise and benediction, where all comes to flower and spreads sweetness and perfume. *Come, my beloved, my dearest, that you may see me more clearly. Come to the window through which I can look upon you. Come, consider my heart in the opening of my side. Come and show me your face. Ah! Now I see it though you know it not, but I shall see it and you shall show it to me for you shall see that I see it. Let me hear your voice, for I wish to incorporate it with mine. So will your face be comely and your voice pleasant and sweet* (cf. Song 2:13–14).

Meditation is simply an attentive thought that is reiterated and deliberately entertained in order to excite the will to holy and salutary affections and resolves. The Sacred Spouse says: *The voice of the turtle dove is heard in our land* (cf. Song 2:12). By this he means that a devout soul is very agreeable to him when she presents herself before him and meditates in order to nourish within herself holy love for him. In this sense the Apostle said: *Think diligently upon him that endured such opposition from sinners against himself that you be not wearied, fainting in your minds* (cf. Heb 12:3).

Oh, how happy are those who with an ever-abiding, wondering admiration utter within themselves these loving words of the great Saint Augustine: *O Beauty ever ancient, ever new;* and those of David: *You are good and in your goodness teach me your justifications* (cf. Ps 119:68). *How sweet are your words to my palate! More than honey to my mouth* (cf. Ps 119:103). Or with Saint Thomas: *My Lord and my God* (cf. Jn 20:28) or with Magdalene: *Rabboni* (cf. Jn 20:16). To be inebriated is to be so in love with the thought of his beauty and so united to his goodness from constant and ardent contemplation as to be carried out of oneself.

Show me, O you whom my soul loves, where you repose, where you lie in the midday (cf. Song 1:7).

See how the beloved contents herself with knowing that her Lover is with her. Oh, truly to be and to wish to be always, for ever and ever, pleasing to God is a good method of keeping one's self in his presence. Now in this state of quiet the will only acts by a simple acquiescence to the divine good pleasure, desiring, in prayer, nothing other than simply to be in God's presence in whatever manner he wills. This is quietude of a supremely excellent character, for it is purified of every interest; the faculties of the soul, nay even the will, take contentment in nothing, if not in being without contentment for the sake of God's contentment; for his good pleasure is her repose. It is the height of loving ecstasy to desire the contentment of God and in no way her own.

— Excerpt from conferences on prayer given
to the Sisters of the Visitation

XII

The Presence of God

O sweet Jesus, draw me always deeper and deeper into your heart, that buried there in your love I may be wholly swallowed up in your sweetness. When the human heart energizes itself with strength in prayer, it transplants itself by heavenly love from this world to God. It will assuredly never cease to stretch forth and bind itself fast to the Divinity, uniting itself more and more closely to his goodness, yet by a growth that is all unperceived until it be accomplished. Oh, how happy is the soul that in tranquility of heart lovingly maintains this holy sentiment of the presence of God! Such a union will perpetually, though insensibly, increase until the spirit is steeped in infinite, loving tranquility.

Now when I speak as I do here of the holy sentiment of the presence of God, I do not mean a sensible presence but that which resides in the highest or supreme point of the spirit, where divine love reigns and chiefly operates. To this union the Divine Shepherd of souls provokes his beloved. *Put me,* he says, *as a seal upon your heart, as a seal upon your arm* (cf. Song 8:6). Thus does he wish our union with him to be so strong, so close that we bear its mark upon us. Ah, Jesus, who will give me the grace that my spirit may be one with yours! Lord, rejecting the multiplicity of created things, I desire only union with you. You are the sole object, the solitary unity essential to my soul!

Swallow up this atom of being that you have given me in the sea of your goodness from which it came. Ah, Lord, since your heart loves mine and I long for you to seize my heart from me, why do you not take it? Draw me and I will run, allured by your attractions, to cast myself into your fatherly arms, never to stir from them, to stay there for ever and ever. Amen.

Our heart is made for God, who continually entices it and does not cease pouring into it the *attrait* [fascination] of his heavenly love, but there are five things that impede the energizing of this holy attraction: sin, the love of riches, sensual pleasures, pride and vanity, and self-love with its multitude of unruly passions, a burden under which we succumb. Whoever truly takes pleasure in God desires to please him and to do this, faithfully conforms herself to him. Truly, the delight of the good God is to be with the children of men, to pour out his graces upon them. O Goodness infinitely sweet, how lovable is your will, how desirable are your favors! You have created me for eternal life. Your sacred breasts are enkindled with a love that admits of no comparison; they abound with the milk of mercy, be it to pardon the penitent or to perfect the just. Ah, why then does our will not cling to you to drink in the milk of eternal benediction as the infant with tenacity suckles at his mother's breast? In order to accomplish this, we must make up our minds to will and to welcome all suitable means and make special resolution on this point. For this David accepted commensurate penance; as for me, I ought to accept abjections, but when we love they are a joy to us.

When charity leads some to a life of poverty, and others to shut themselves up in cloisters, no one has a right to demand its reasons. If its actions are called in question it answers boldly: It is because the *Lord has need of them* (cf. Mt 21:3). All should be at the service of charity but she is at the service of no one, not even of her Beloved, for she is not his servant but his spouse, since it is not service but love she renders him. O Lord, let me never offend you in anything; grant that my will may never be other than your will. Great souls do everything they can to be pleasing to God.

— Excerpt from conferences on prayer given
to the Sisters of the Visitation

XIII

The Ardor of Love

Speaking to her Daughters on various degrees of prayer, and the conditions required for progress in prayer, Saint Jane says:

God wills that we should have spiritual enemies and he wills that we should resist them; between these two divine wills let us live courageously. We should suffer assaults with patience, and valiantly strive to withstand them. She who when praying is conscious that she prays is not perfectly attentive to her prayer, for she diverts her attention from God to whom she is praying to the prayer she is addressing to him. Even the care we take to avoid distractions often serves as the greatest distraction.

Simplicity in spiritual actions is highly commendable. If you turn your eyes upon yourself it is no longer God whom you look upon, but your own attitude with regard to him. Fervent prayer makes no return to the self; it is occupied with God alone. Such is the ardor of holy love.

When the tumult of spiritual troubles deprives us of every other kind of alleviation and every means of resistance, let us recommend our spirit to the care of Jesus Christ who is our true Father and, bowing our head to his good pleasure, consign to him our whole will. We must faithfully employ our time, like Job, in blessing him for all he does. How admirable is this occupation of our will when it leaves the care of willing and choosing—the disposal of all things—to God, with praise and thanksgiving for every issue. Often say: My Father loves me truly and I, I am all his.

When love enters into a soul it makes it happy to die to self to live again to God, for it despoils it of all natural desires and of that self-love which clings as closely to the spirit as the skin does to the flesh. Then God strips it of the most laudable affections, such as those it had to spiritual consolations, to exercises of piety, to the perfection of virtues, which seemed to be the very life of the devout soul (cf. Saint John of the Cross, *Dark Night of the Soul*, Book II: Chapter 3: Section 3).

Yes, the same Lord who in the beginning gave us the desire for the attainment of virtues and made us practice them on every occasion now takes from us all such affections, that with the greater tranquility, purity, and simplicity we may have no loving desire for anything save his Divine Majesty's sweet will.

With peace of mind, with calm serenity, we ought to see ourselves reclothed in our misery and abjection, therein to abide in the midst of our imperfections and feebleness until God exalts us to the practice of more excellent virtues. She who leaves all for God should take back nothing except such as God wills her to have again. She no longer nourishes her body save to serve the spirit as God wishes; she no longer studies save to serve her neighbor and her own soul according to the divine intention. She no longer practices virtues because they are to her liking, but because God desires it. Just so, therefore, must we denude ourselves of all affections, little and great, and often examine our heart to see if it is ready to strip itself, as Isaiah said: then again, to reclothe itself in due time with affections befitting the service of charity. In a word, we must die on the cross, all naked, with our Divine Savior and arise afterward as a new creation with him. When we think of our neighbor created in the image and likeness of God we ought to say to one another: Look, see this creature, how she resembles her Creator. Should we not embrace her, caress her, be full of affection for her, call down upon her a thousand blessings? Ah, not for the love of her, because we do not know if she is in herself worthy of love or hatred. Then why? Oh, for the love of God who has created her in his own image and thereby renders her capable of participating in his goodness, his grace and glory. For love of God, I say, by whom she is, to whom she is, through whom she is, in whom she is, and for whom she is; to whom she has a resemblance in a unique manner. This resemblance is why divine love so often not only commands the love of our neighbor, but also creates that love and diffuses it in the human heart, and she in whom this love is diffused would willingly die to save her neighbor from perishing. True zeal has a glowing ardor but it is constant, firm, sweet, laborious, equally lovable and indefatigable. All otherwise is false zeal; it is turbulent, disordered, insolent, proud, short-lived, angry, equally impetuous and inconstant.

Of all virtuous actions we ought most carefully to practice those of religion and of reverence toward divine things, those of faith, of hope, and of most holy fear of God. We should often speak of heavenly things, thinking of and longing for eternity, frequenting churches and the divine services, reading devout books, observing the ceremonies of religion, for all these exercises feed the desire of holy love and diffuse its graces more abundantly.

— Excerpt from conferences on prayer given
to the Sisters of the Visitation

XIV

Drawn to Simplicity

Rules given by Saint Jane to her Daughters to help them discern if it is the Spirit of God that operates in their souls when they cannot pray or meditate:

You ask me, my Daughter, how we are to know if the inability to actively meditate is brought about by God drawing the soul to simplicity and tranquility in his presence. According to the teaching of the masters of the spiritual life there are three signs by which we may know.

The first sign that God is drawing the soul to a more quiet prayer is if she can no longer meditate or finds nothing but aridity in meditation, and if the mind notwithstanding her efforts comes back always to the same subject.

There is no doubt that this difficulty of not being able to make considerations leads to a more simple prayer. No matter how faintly the soul may feel herself growing in tranquility and in an attitude of reverence before God, this feeling ought, nonetheless, to strengthen her in the way to which God is now undoubtedly calling her. She should not give up her prayer although she is spiritually poverty-stricken and suffers from distractions, but let her patiently and peacefully remain before God without voluntarily giving way to distractions (cf. *On the Love of God*, Book 6: Chapter 9).

The second sign is if meditation using the imagination and senses on any given subject no longer attracts us and does not serve as any help towards the practice of virtue.

The third—and the surest—sign is this: the soul takes pleasure in being alone, praying by means of a simple, loving attention to God, in inward peace, quiet, and repose, making no particular considerations in prayer, but instead preferring to remain in a state of general loving attentiveness (cf. Saint John of the Cross, *The Ascent of Mount Carmel*, Book II: Chapter 13: Section 4).

Before giving up meditation to enter into this prayer of attentiveness to the presence of God, a soul should manifest these three signs together. If the soul is really drawn to this simple attention, though she seems to occupy herself in nothing at prayer and make no use of the senses, let her not fear to lose herself or think that the time so spent is useless, for though the [other] powers of the soul cease to act the intelligence remains. In short, when the action of grace is confined to our intelligence the understanding may be inactive in regard to all special things, temporal or spiritual, and the will may have no inclination to dwell on them. However, when grace is communicated to the will, which in a greater or lesser degree it [almost] always is, the soul does not cease to hear, to consider, to attend to her occupations, to unite herself to the divine action, even so far as to lose herself therein. She is carried away by love to such an extent as to be unable to render any account to herself as to whether she understands or whether she loves.

Most willingly will I give you some signs by which you shall know if your repose and quietude at prayer are good and God-given.

It is a sign from God if you find that this attraction leads to lowliness and contempt of earthly things.

If you are led to make a better manifestation of yourself to your superiors, to be very simple, sincere, upright, candid; or in other words, to be like a little child.

If, notwithstanding the graciousness you receive from this sweet repose, you are ready, should God so will, to resume again the use of the imagination, of considerations, and yes, even to bear aridity.

If you are more patient and more humble in suffering your infirmities. Still better, if your desire for suffering increases, regardless of relief, or contentment other than the happiness of giving pleasure to your Spouse.

Scan briefly and in a general way your attraction and quiet prayer to see if they do not make the world, personal vanity, and self-interest seem more contemptible. In a word, if you learn from them to trample underfoot all earthly glories and even your own self, if they teach you to prize contempt, abjection, pain, and the cross more than anything else. And moreover, my dear Daughter, this I maintain: your attraction is undoubtedly good and it is from God. Do not be anxious about the nourishment of your soul, for this quietness is worth more than all other meats, and although it seems to you that your soul is slumbering, believe me it is not without nourishment; it is partaking of good and delicious food.

But being so completely taken up with the love of Jesus, upon which you feast, it takes no notice of other banquets that he provides for it, and so it must be, or else the soul puts herself in danger of falling from her place.

— Excerpts from rules on prayer given
to the Sisters of the Visitation, from an
undated letter written to a Visitation Sister

XV

The Attentiveness of Love

In this state God is the principal agent who prepares and teaches; the soul is she who receives the spiritual gifts that are given: attention and divine love united in one. Now since his goodness from that time on acts upon the soul as a Giver, she ought to go to God with a trustful heart, doing nothing in prayer except that for which he gives her an attraction. She should remain quite passive, in no way energizing herself, looking to God with the quiet simplicity of a child, thus with simple attention joining love with love. If the soul wishes to go forth from this very simple, loving, tranquil, inarticulate attention, her action puts a stop to the good things that God communicates through this mere attention that he requires of her. Hence she ought to be free, detached, passive, and calm, like God, for in order to receive these divine operations the mind must be utterly detached and profoundly humble. If the soul wishes to lean upon some thought, some discourse, some consolation and to meditate particularly on this, it will only serve to distract her and to turn her away from the deep utterance to which God gives voice in the very core of her heart. For in this sacred solitude all the faculties should be in silence, peace, and tranquility that the soul may hear what he has to say.

Now, inasmuch as this peace speaks within her, when the soul feels herself drawn into a listening silence her loving regard must be quite simple, without either solicitude or reflection, insomuch that she forgets everything in her desire to give her attention, so she may be free to do what grace makes known to her.

Note, my Daughter, once the soul begins to enter into this simple and inactive state she ought not at any time or season to apply herself to meditation, nor should she expect spiritual lights or consolations, but she should remain standing, as it were at attention, without support, the mind free of desire of any good thing present or absent. For it is impossible that this elevated wisdom can be received save by a singular detachment from consolations and from all special affections. Keep your soul in freedom, in peace, in calm; detached from the sweetness and the servitude of its works. Do not let it worry about any care or solicitude, high or low. Make the soul a captive to solitude, for the sooner it abstains from such things the more fully will it enter into this holy inaction and tranquility.

— Excerpt from rules on prayer
given to the Sisters of the Visitation

XVI

God Alone

*Saint Jane's words to a soul desiring to be led by the way of
simplicity and of complete detachment, addressed to and col-
lected by one of the first Mothers of the Visitation Order. They
reveal the attitudes of Saint Jane, as she says that these were
the counsels she received at a time she herself was suffering
from bitter spiritual trials:*

God wills you to be in an extremely passive state, giving no thought to your future perseverance or to your
present fidelity and acceptability to God. Empty yourself
of self and of all solicitude, all apprehension, all bore-
dom, all dread of a prolongation of this state wherein
everything gives pain and is done with fear. This simple

regard [this looking to God] with unquestioning obedience will be your safeguard. I tell you again on the part of God, you are too introspective. Do not put yourself in any more pain regarding your pain. Speak of it neither to God nor within yourself. Never reflect on it or think how to express yourself about it to anyone whatsoever, and make no examination upon it. Hide your pain from yourself and look to God as if you did not feel it. If you speak to him let it be of himself and not of your trouble.

Lifting your eyes to heaven with a trustful smile, be content with saying: O Eternity! Eternity! Read sometimes the sixty-fifth letter of the fourth book which our blessed Father once wrote to me.[1] Abide submissively in the will of God's good pleasure, which impoverishes you and strips you of every manner of inward satisfaction, having taken from you all knowledge of the blessings and gifts that are yours through his grace. His goodness has infused these good things into your soul in such a manner that they are inseparable from your inward life. But the Divine Guide, to raise you to a higher perfection, has taken from you your faith, your hope in him, your love of his goodness, your trust, the sense of abandonment, and

---

1. This letter, dated March 28, 1612, and often recommended to others by Saint Jane, includes advice from Saint Francis de Sales on how to persevere in interior darkness.

the repose you have had in him, together with all the inward faculties of your soul and the precious gifts he had conferred upon you.

All this he has taken and thrown into the crucible, into the fire of his most pure and divine love. Every pleasure, satisfaction, and contentment he has thus consumed and annihilated in you. Moreover, he has done this not only as regards earthly things, for that was accomplished long ago, but the Divine Master also wishes to annihilate in you the very pleasure that you have taken in the graces with which he has endowed you. As he gave them so now he has, as regards feeling, deprived you of them, for he wants your soul to be occupied not with his gifts but with himself alone. God, having taken from you all knowledge, perception, realization of these things, having made you a beggar, will have you abide in patience and submission to his good pleasure. You will abide without desire, sight, knowledge (herein is the test of your faith), or any other virtue, relish, satisfaction, sensible devotion, or sentiment, whatever it may be: in short, without any graces. Content yourself that God has all these things in himself and that, maintaining yourself united to him, you possess all that is in him.

Above all, never deliberately lose your time in thinking how you are united to God, or comment within yourself upon your submission, abandonment, or confidence. Let it be enough for you that he knows and sees and that at present all he wishes of you is the patient abiding with peace and quiet in him, by this simple looking to him and drawing unto him as far as you are able, while his divine operations are taking place within you.

As to knowing if this state will last long, leave that to God, without desiring to be delivered from it or seeking to inquire into its duration, remaining submissive even should it please his goodness to keep you in it till the judgment. Now amid all this anguish your only fear is that of offending him, of not giving him pleasure, of not being able to serve and glorify him for all eternity. But I assure you on the part of God, to whom you have consecrated yourself for so long a time, that this state is more agreeable to him than if you were raised in rapture to the third heaven and in the possession of all the virtues, joys, and sentiments of which he has now deprived you. For in reality and in substance you have all these virtues, though you have not the knowledge or the realization of them. Hence you have them all the more purely and perfectly and in a far higher degree, inasmuch as they are apart from all sensible consolations. The more completely they are lost to your senses the more precious they are in God's eyes by your humble submission to his divine will, which makes you thus die to self, incapable of any utterance, unless it be, *All is consummated* (cf. Jn 19:30). My God, I have delivered over my whole being into your blessed hands to dispose of as you please. To you I consign the care of my interior life. Govern it according to your good pleasure. For myself I ask only to abide faithfully in patience and to keep my mind on this very simple and unique looking unto you without allowing my mind to roam elsewhere.

— Excerpt from words addressed to one
of the first Mothers of the Visitation Order

XVII

To Possess God

Saint Jane's advice to a soul suffering from spiritual trials:

Remain, I beg of you, unshaken in the assurance I give you on God's part that your faith, hope, and charity are more alive and more perfect than they have ever been. Think no more whether you possess them or possess any virtue. With a mental loving glance at your resolutions, abide in this surety. Carefully avoid any desire to be delivered from your trouble and deprivation. It is a grace that God gives you in order to perfect in you all virtues. It is a reward and not a chastisement. Have no doubt of this.

God wills that you should bear this trial patiently, in absolute submission to him, without allowing your mind to seek either sight or knowledge of what is passing within you. Forbid all disputation or reflections on your temptations whatever they are, and do not ask yourself why this trial is given you. Make no effort to analyze or to subdue your sufferings, temptations, troubles, sorrows, darkness, obscurity, anxieties, embarrassments, extravagant thoughts, or anything whatsoever that exists or passes in your inner life, however painful and tormenting it may be. Neither get alarmed, or be surprised, or voluntarily make any reflections thereon, and do all this absolutely, with no reservation. Regard them all as cruel temptations, hold yourself above them, feign not to see them, however keenly you may feel them. Speak of them neither to God nor to yourself. Look at God and let him act. This alone is all you have to do, and this is the only exercise God requires of you and to which he attracts you. And besides, this is what our blessed Father invariably commanded me to practice and which I, on his part, recommend to you.

Entertain no desire to see, to feel, or to meditate actively, but abide in tranquility, repose, trust, and patience in his presence. Give no thought to see how you are there, or what the soul is doing, has done or will do, or what will happen to it in any occurrence or event whatsoever. It must be absolutely immovable, must not stir, for this unique perception of God (*regard en Dieu*) comprises all and more especially in regard to suffering. You know this very well, and I, likewise, assure you of it. Remain then steadfast in this simplicity, and as soon as you perceive your mind going from it gently bring it back, without act, look, or reflection. *One thing only is necessary* to possess God.

Continue your communions and usual spiritual exercises, making no reflections how you perform them, and leave the care of your salvation and of your inner life to the guidance of God, as well as all else that concerns you. You have sacrificed everything and given all to him; leave to him the care of all. Amen.

— Excerpt from words addressed to one of
the first Mothers of the Visitation Order

XVIII

Return to God

Speaking to her Daughters on distractions in prayer and the presence of God, Saint Jane says:

There is no doubt that a soul who all day long is resisting useless thoughts and who when she becomes conscious of them straightway brings her mind back to God (herein is true virtue) does much more for God than another who has great facility in turning to God and in rejecting all that is irrelevant. Let such souls with courage, faithfulness, and constancy keep to this practice of returning to God, for I assure them it is the real way of acquiring perfection in a short time.

All the Fathers of the Church agree that there is no better occupation in the spiritual life [than the presence of God]; they themselves practiced it. This life-giving presence should, however, be accompanied by death-blows to self. The two exercises ought to go hand in hand. Presence of God and mortification mutually sustain one another. A mortified soul is more susceptible to, more easily permeated by, the divine presence. She has fewer distractions, she does not indulge in wandering thoughts, she tastes God, she keeps herself closely united to him; and the enjoyment of this access to him makes it easy to die to self, while the fortitude that comes of it enables her effectually to overcome or to mitigate difficulties and to endure all with comparative ease.

Saint Jane tells her Daughters that, in order not to lose inward peace, they must do as Saint Francis de Sales says, "Go to God without reflecting on their trouble":

Our way is to make known the reason of our failure and all that was said to us. In a word, we make many useless excuses that are absolutely contrary to the simplicity so strongly recommended by our blessed Father. You are suffering from a little pain, you make a blunder, you have been ruffled; overlook it, pass on to God regardless of your trouble. You say: But I want to look at it so that I may offer it to God. That is good, yet in offering do not magnify it by making reflections that bring you to the conclusion that you have good reason to complain. Ah, truly we must be more generous, putting our satisfaction solely in God and abandoning ourselves absolutely to him, who is our only desire. Believe me, Daughters, a simple soul is a confident soul; she trusts in God and has nothing to fear. But there are times when all seems lost, everything appears to go wrong; without confidence at such times where should we then be? Like Abraham, we must hope against hope and, recommending everything to God, abide in peace, never ceasing to trust in his sweet Providence, for it will take care of us.

I know of no greater happiness than that of the recollected soul, the soul of prayer who knows how to act with God. She has found, our blessed Father used to say, the sacred alchemy that changes all her miseries into the gold of a most ardent charity, and of lasting heavenly consolations. She experiences that there is no joy to equal the joy of living with God alone, she and God alone, detached from all created things.

— Excerpts from a conference given to the Sisters of the Visitation; and *Paroles Consolantes* ("Words of Consolation"), addressed to the Sisters of the Visitation

XIX

Lost in God

On the loss of self in God Saint Jane says:

I see by what you say, my dear Sisters, that you wish to lose yourselves in God. To be lost in God is nothing else than to be absolutely and wholly resigned and given over into his hands, surrendered to the care of his adorable Providence. These words, *to be lost in God*, bear a certain significance which I think can only be understood by those who are thus happily lost.

The great Saint Paul understood it well when he said: *I live now not I but Christ lives in me* (cf. Gal 2:20). Oh, my Sisters, how happy should we be could we truly say: It is no more I who live in me because my whole life is lost in God. It is he who lives through me and in me. To live no longer in oneself, to be lost in God, is the most sublime perfection the soul can attain. Yet to this perfection we must all aspire, losing ourselves again and again a thousand times in the ocean of his infinite greatness. Now a soul thus lost is always reduced to a sense of annihilation before God. However God may treat her inwardly or outwardly, she is content; nothing happens to her that does not give her satisfaction; she welcomes affliction and looks upon it unmoved because she says: In me the consolation of being lost in God extinguishes all other consolations. . . .

Now we desire to lose ourselves in God, but at the same time we desire that this losing of ourselves may not entail much suffering. We tell our Lord indeed that we surrender ourselves into his divine arms, yet we have not done it the right way, for we want to have some little say in it ourselves, not perhaps so much in temporal matters as in spiritual. Self-love, with its subtle finesse, is ever persuading us that if we have no hand in it, all will not go well.

A soul completely *lost* in God has no wish for any virtue, any perfection, save only what God wishes her to have. She works hard to attain virtue because God so wishes, but she leaves to him the results of her labor and does not trouble to find new means of arriving at perfection; she confines herself to make good use of those at hand, those put in her way by Providence.

It is, my Sisters, quite true that although we may have given ourselves to God completely we may easily take ourselves back again. Now what are we to do in this case? Humble ourselves genuinely and acknowledge that we are not so completely lost in God since we have been so prompt in finding ourselves again. Having made this act of profound humility we should again lose ourselves into God as a little drop of water into the sea, and lose ourselves so securely in this ocean of Divine Goodness as never again to find ourselves.

Every time that you find you have thus taken yourself back, once again faithfully restore yourself to God, and if you persevere loyally in this practice, I dare to promise you that you will with such a happy *loss* lose yourself at last in God as never again to find yourself.

— Excerpt from a conference given
to the Sisters of the Visitation

Bibliography

Francis de Sales and Jane Frances de Chantal, *Letters of Spiritual Direction*, translated by Péronne Marie Thibert, V.H.M. New York: Paulist Press, 1988.

Jane Frances de Chantal, *The Spirit of Saint Jane Frances de Chantal as Shown by Her Letters*, translated by the Sisters of the Visitation. New York: Longmans, Green, and Co., 1922.

Jane Frances de Chantal, *The Spiritual Life: A Summary of the Instructions on the Virtues and on Prayer*, compiled by the Sisters of the Visitation. St. Louis, Missouri: B. Herder Book Co., 1928.

Jane Frances de Chantal, *St. Chantal on Prayer: A translation of her writings on prayer*, translated by Rev. A. Durand, Ph.D. Boston, Massachusetts: St. Paul Editions (Pauline Books & Media), 1968.

Wendy M. Wright, *Bond of Perfection: Jeanne de Chantal & François de Sales*. New York: Paulist Press, 1985.

BOOKS & MEDIA

A mission of the Daughters of St. Paul

As apostles of Jesus Christ, evangelizing today's world:

We are CALLED to holiness
by God's living Word and Eucharist.

We COMMUNICATE the Gospel message
through our lives and through all
available forms of media.

We SERVE the Church
by responding to the hopes and needs
of all people with the Word of God,
in the spirit of St. Paul.

For more information visit our Web site:
www.pauline.org.

BOOKS & MEDIA

The Daughters of St. Paul operate book and media centers at the following addresses. Visit, call, or write the one nearest you today, or find us on the World Wide Web, www.pauline.org.

CALIFORNIA

3908 Sepulveda Blvd, Culver City, CA 90230	310-397-8676
935 Brewster Avenue, Redwood City, CA 94063	650-369-4230
5945 Balboa Avenue, San Diego, CA 92111	858-565-9181

FLORIDA

145 S.W. 107th Avenue, Miami, FL 33174	305-559-6715

HAWAII

1143 Bishop Street, Honolulu, HI 96813	808-521-2731
Neighbor Islands call:	866-521-2731

ILLINOIS

172 North Michigan Avenue, Chicago, IL 60601	312-346-4228

LOUISIANA

4403 Veterans Memorial Blvd, Metairie, LA 70006	504-887-7631

MASSACHUSETTS

885 Providence Hwy, Dedham, MA 02026	781-326-5385

MISSOURI

9804 Watson Road, St. Louis, MO 63126	314-965-3512

NEW YORK

64 W. 38th Street, New York, NY 10018	212-754-1110

PENNSYLVANIA

Philadelphia—relocating	215-676-9494

SOUTH CAROLINA

243 King Street, Charleston, SC 29401	843-577-0175

VIRGINIA

1025 King Street, Alexandria, VA 22314	703-549-3806

CANADA

3022 Dufferin Street, Toronto, ON M6B 3T5	416-781-9131

¡También somos su fuente para libros, videos y música en español!